High Voice

15 EASY
SPIRITUAL
ARRANGEMENTS
FOR THE PROGRESSING SINGER

EDITED BY RICHARD WALTERS

ISBN 978-0-634-09845-1

HAL•LEONARD®
CORPORATION

7777 W. BLUEMOUND RD. P.O. BOX 13819 MILWAUKEE, WI 53213

In Australia Contact:
Hal Leonard Australia Pty. Ltd.
4 Lentara Court
Cheltenham, Victoria, 3192 Australia
Email: ausadmin@halleonard.com.au

Visit Hal Leonard Online at
www.halleonard.com

CONTENTS

Singers on the recordings: * Tanya Kruse, soprano, ** Steven Stolen, tenor
Pianists on the recordings: + Brian Dean, ++ Christopher Ruck, +++ Richard Walters

PREFACE

When Richard Walters compiled the book *15 Easy Folksong Arrangements*, he asked me to write the Preface. This publication, *15 Easy Spiritual Arrangements*, follows along the same parameters as the folksong volume. Again, I am delighted to write some introductory remarks for this volume.

Spirituals are so much a part of our cultural heritage that our young singers should include them as part of their singing repertoire. The singing of spirituals represents the feelings of the heart and inner self in a way no other repertoire is capable of doing. In expressing the sufferings of slavery, the rhythms of physical work, the jubilant faith in God, the sadness, grief, and longings for freedom, singers learn to tap into their feelings of expressiveness and compassion. For many years, people considered spirituals to be entirely the domain of African-American singers. However, I believe that these songs are testimonies of a people, representing an important American folk heritage, and need to be shared by singers of all races.

These new arrangements provide freshness and simplicity to these collections for high and low voice. The arrangements are completely accessible for most student pianists. The vocal ranges are very moderate, not going above F for high voice and not going above D for low voice. The spirituals chosen are among the best known of the genre.

The companion recordings include professionally sung performances, offering ideas for vocal interpretations. They should be used primarily as a listening guide, not to be imitated. The recorded accompaniments are an aid in practicing for students who do not have an accompanist available. The accompaniments are best used with a teacher's guidance, pointing out that other tempos and expressive possibilities, different from the recordings, are available to individual singers in live performances.

The students I have introduced to the *15 Easy Folksong Arrangements* have had much success with the songs, and I have no doubt that many students of mine will find this spirituals volume just as satisfying. In addition, beginning adult singers will discover a sense of enjoyment as they successfully tackle these familiar tunes. And, of course, these spirituals make excellent church service solos for any singer.

Joan Frey Boytim
June, 2005

ABOUT SPIRITUALS

Being held captive for life, forced into labor, torn from family and friends forever at the whim of an owner. These were the everyday realities of the African-American slave. It was a life of extreme hardship, often in terrible conditions. Not only did this beastly situation lead slaves to despair, but often a premature death. African-American slaves aurally learned English from their masters and from one another, and also took the Christian religion as their own. Uneducated and illiterate (it was illegal for slaves to learn to read), they learned the Bible from sermons and conversations. Slaves naturally identified with the Jews of the Old Testament who were delivered from bondage in Egypt. Like the Jews, the African-American slaves believed that they were "chosen" to be liberated. Spirituals arose as an expression of emotion and religion, a type of slave song that was sung in Sunday worship, "camp-meetings," and in the daily life of work and social gatherings.

The writers of spirituals are not known. Just as a story changes in its telling, passed on from one person to another, spirituals altered as they were passed down from one singer to another, from one generation to another. This is a common feature of all folk music. Slaves who were sold to a new master might have brought previously unknown songs and spirituals to the culture of a plantation. Slaves accompanying masters on a visit to a neighboring plantation might have had the opportunity to sing songs with resident slaves, thereby spreading a common knowledge of spirituals. There is also considerable evidence that there was musical interchange between rural white churches and slaves, both groups learning from one another.

Spirituals existed perhaps as early as the 17th century. There are references to the genre in writings of the 18th and 19th centuries, but there is no published evidence of actual songs until the later 1800s. One of the earliest music publications of spirituals was *Slave Songs of the United States* (1867) by Allen, Ware and Garrison. It is certainly significant that this was published two years after the abolition of slavery; its publication before that time would have probably been unlikely. In this collection, the authors state that all the spirituals were transcribed from live performances heard on plantations, on river levees, riverboats, or sung by prison laborers. The spirituals included in *Slave Songs* were identified from different regions of the south. However, none of what became the most famous spirituals, such as those in this collection, were included in this historical publication.

Many spirituals draw their texts from Bible stories. They sometimes are based on *The Book of Revelation* with its declaration of the return of Jesus Christ, an obvious symbol of hope. Besides being emotional and religious expression, spirituals acted as a form of coded communication between slaves, even in the presence of slave-owners. In "Didn't My Lord Deliver Daniel?," "Canaan" refers to the northern free states or Canada (also referred to as "heaven"). The deep south was often called "hell," and "Pharaoh" was the slave-owner. Many songs speak of escape from bondage, either through the end of enslavement, or through death. In "Swing Low, Sweet Chariot" and "Gospel Train," the "chariot" and "train" most likely refer to the Underground Railroad, a secret network established to move slaves to freedom in the north. The "Jordan River" symbolized the Ohio River, the dividing boundary between the slave-holding south and the free north. Many songs had a double meaning of earthly and spiritual freedom. "Steal Away" not only refers to an obvious escape from bondage, but also the spiritual liberation gained in the next life.

"Sorrow songs" are spirituals of a sad nature, with texts that emotionally reflect the downtrodden life of a slave, identifying with the misunderstood and unjustly abused Jesus. "Were You There?" and "Sometimes I Feel Like a Motherless Child" are such songs. One reason the melodies of spirituals seem so pure is that there was no tradition of part-singing among the slaves by all accounts. Intensely emotional and expressive group singing in unison was the style. The secular "blues" may well have roots in these sorrow song spirituals. Upbeat, rhythmic spirituals were called "jubilees," which were sometimes accompanied by dancing, hand-clapping and improvised percussion. "Every Time I Feel the Spirit" and "He's Got the Whole World in His Hands" (though in a slower, more soulful arrangement in this collection) are good examples of this positive type of jubilee spiritual. Syncopation is common in both slow and fast spirituals, and is an obvious root of ragtime and early jazz. In the 1920s the genre of gospel music grew directly out of the jubilee gospel tradition. Rhythm and Blues, and its successor, Rock 'n' Roll, have clear, identifiable roots in the spiritual.

Spirituals were rural music of the south. Although they began as a type of folk song, spirituals became known throughout the world when adapted to traditional concert venues. The Jubilee Singers from Fisk University of Nashville was one of the first ensembles to tour with spirituals to paying audiences in northern American and European cities, a historically important 1871 tour to raise money for the school founded to educate freed slaves. Due to stylistic but fully composed, published arrangements by Clarence Cameron White, William Grant Still, T.P. Fenner, Nathaniel Dett and Frederick J. Work, spirituals were heard in performances by every type of ensemble in the late 19th and early 20th centuries. Prominent African-American composers who brought the spiritual into the concert hall for solo singer and piano, in the tradition of art song, were Harry T. Burleigh and Hall Johnson. Famous performers such as Marian Anderson and Paul Robeson sang spirituals in recital around the world, sometimes with added political meaning in civil rights contexts. Many spirituals have long been adapted for hymnals of almost every church denomination, and are regularly sung by congregations in services internationally, reaching millions of people.

Spirituals are for all singers, not just those of African-American origin. They represent a significant part of historical American folk music. Beyond educational use, it goes without saying that spirituals make excellent church solos.

For this edition, we have eliminated much of the dialect, using standard English instead, which we believe serves most singers. If you are comfortable as a performer with dialect appropriate to the southern, rural language of spirituals, feel free to add your interpretation to the words and diction. As to performance, don't make the mistake of missing the emotional core of this music. A rendition that is too cool in its temperament is not likely to find the heart of a spiritual.

ABOUT THE RECORDINGS AND ARRANGEMENTS

Even though this material is designed primarily for first and second year voice students, we deliberately chose to record the performances with professional singers at a high level of development, rather than recording young, student voices. Hearing a real singer phrase and express a piece of music is excellent instruction. It also may inspire you, and fire your imagination.

A gifted singer has vibrato in his or her voice naturally. It is part of the color of an individual voice. Instrumentalists sometimes do not understand this, because wind and string players have to work at learning how to create vibrato in their playing, which is actually an imitation of singing. In your choral experience as a singer a director may have asked specifically for a "pure tone" without vibrato at times. But for solo classical singing, and for those in traditional voice lessons, vibrato is a natural part of opening up the voice. This is important to understand for those young or inexperienced persons just becoming familiar with classical singing. The singers on the recordings are doing nothing deliberate regarding vibrato. They are just singing in a healthy, supported manner with their natural vocal sound, just as you should do with your own voice.

We urge you not to imitate the performances on the recordings. Do not attempt to imitate their tone or the details of their performances. These recordings are for familiarizing you with the songs and arrangements. It is very important for you to come up with your own interpretation. You can only do this after you know the song very well, and have experimented with different ways of phrasing, worked on diction, and pondered the words of a song. Your teacher will undoubtedly help you with interpretation.

We necessarily must choose one tempo in recording a piano accompaniment track for you to use in your practice. Our choice of tempo, phrasing, *ritardandos*, and dynamics is carefully considered, usually played by the arranger himself in the case of *15 Easy Spiritual Arrangements*. But by the nature of recording, it is only one choice. You may find in working with a pianist that you need a slightly faster or slower tempo than on the recordings, and you also may have your own interpretive ideas that differ from our recordings.

Companion recordings such as this are best used with the guidance of a voice teacher, who can help point out to you things you may need to do to accommodate your voice and singing.

These spiritual arrangements were created with the progressing voice in mind. The ranges are modest, as are the musical issues addressed. We tried to treat this work more as organic composition, with all the values of full composition, rather than an approach to arranging that harmonizes a melody. The accompaniments should be accessible to intermediate student pianists.

We aimed to create useful and expressive arrangements that will hold up as musically substantial even for more experienced singers. Our wish is that you may inspire others in your singing of them.

Balm in Gilead

African-American Spiritual
arranged by Christopher Ruck

then the Ho - ly Spir - it re - vives my soul a - gain. _____

poco rit.

Tempo I

There _ is a balm in Gil - e - ad to make the wound - ed

poco rit. **a tempo**

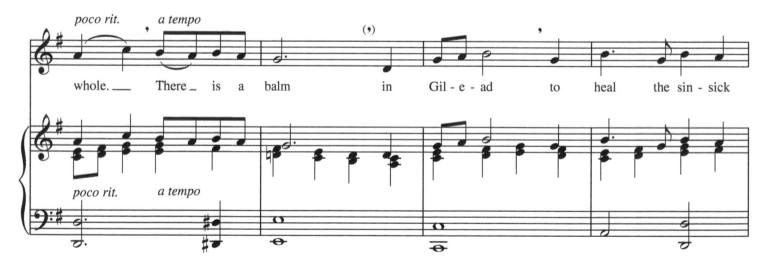

whole. __ There _ is a balm in Gil - e - ad to heal the sin - sick

A little faster

soul. If you can - not preach like

Pe - ter, if you can - not pray like Paul, you can tell the love of Je - sus and

Tempo I

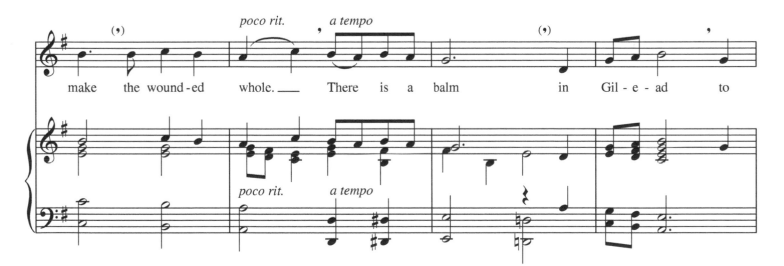

say, "He died for all." ___ There _ is a balm in Gil - e - ad to

make the wound - ed whole. ___ There is a balm in Gil - e - ad to

heal the sin - sick soul, to heal the sin - sick soul. _____

Didn't My Lord Deliver Daniel?

African-American Spiritual
arranged by Brian Dean

Dan - iel, _____ then why not ev - er - y man?

1. He de -
2. The

liv - ered Dan - iel from the li - on's den, Jo - nah from the bel - ly of the
wind blow east and the wind blow west, blow like the Judge - ment _____

whale. And the He - brew chil - dren from the fier - y fur - nace, then
Day, and ev - 'ry soul that nev - er did pray will be

why not ev - er - y man? day.
glad to pray _ that

3. I

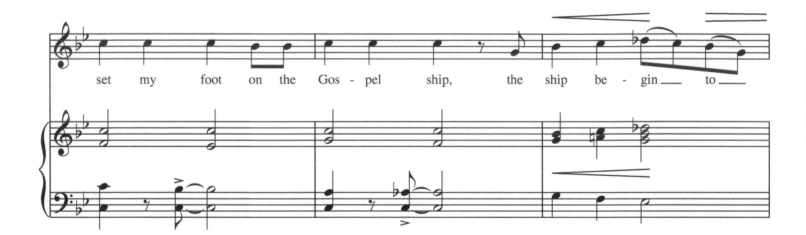

set my foot on the Gos - pel ship, the ship be - gin to

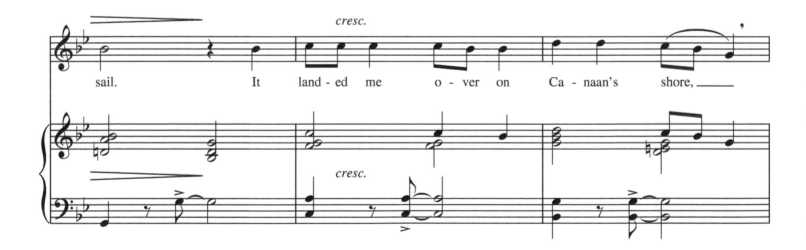

sail. It land - ed me o - ver on Ca - naan's shore,

nev - er come back no more.

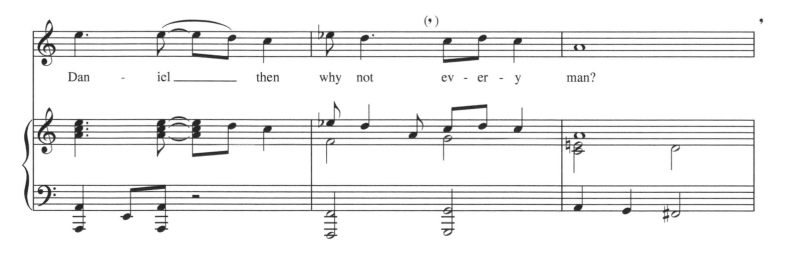

Every Time I Feel the Spirit

African-American Spiritual
arranged by Brian Dean

in my heart, _____ I will pray.

1. Up - on the
2. The Jor - dan

moun - tain _____ when my Lord spoke, out of his
Riv - er _____ is chilly and cold, it chills the

mouth came _____ fire and smoke. I looked a - round me, _____ it looked so
bod - y, _____ not the soul. There ain' but one train _____ up - on this

fine, and I asked my Lord _____ if all was mine. Ev - 'ry
track, it runs to heav - en _____ and then right

18

back. Ev - 'ry time I _____ feel the Spir - it _____ mov - in'

in my heart, ____ I will pray. Yes, ev - 'ry time I _____ feel the

Spir - it, _____ mov - in' in my heart, _____ I will

pray, mov - in' in my heart, _____ I will pray.

Jacob's Ladder

African-American Spiritual
arranged by Richard Walters

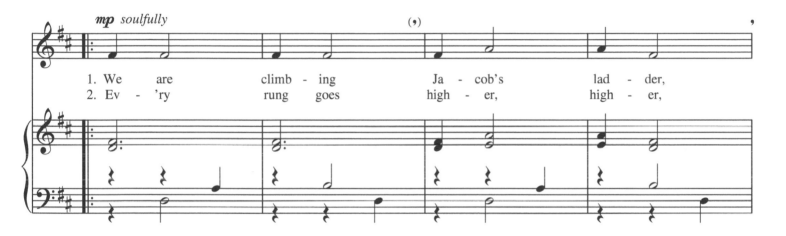

1. We are climb - ing Ja - cob's lad - der,
2. Ev - 'ry rung goes high - er, high - er,

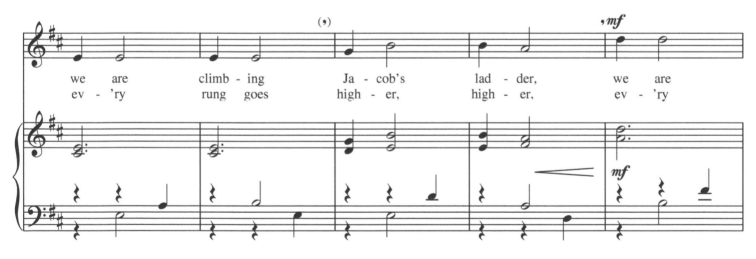

we are climb - ing Ja - cob's lad - der, we are
ev - 'ry rung goes high - er, high - er, ev - 'ry

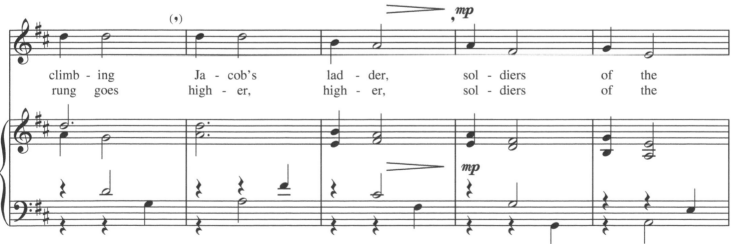

climb - ing Ja - cob's lad - der, sol - diers of the
rung goes high - er, high - er, sol - diers of the

cross.
cross.

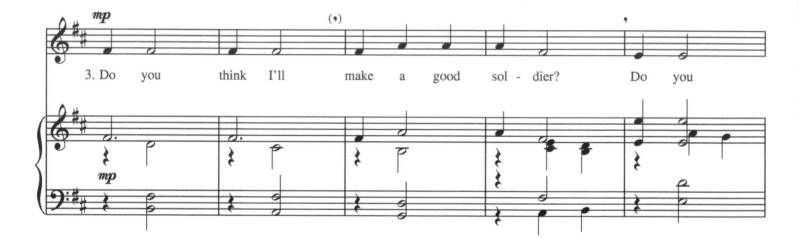

3. Do you think I'll make a good sol - dier? Do you

think I'll make a good sol - dier? Do you think I'll

make a good sol - dier, sol - dier of the cross?

4. Rise, shine,
give God the glo - ry. Rise, shine,
give God the glo - ry. Rise, shine, give God the
glo - ry, sol - diers of the cross.

Go, Tell It on the Mountain

Verses by John W. Work, Jr

African-American Spiritual
arranged by Brian Dean

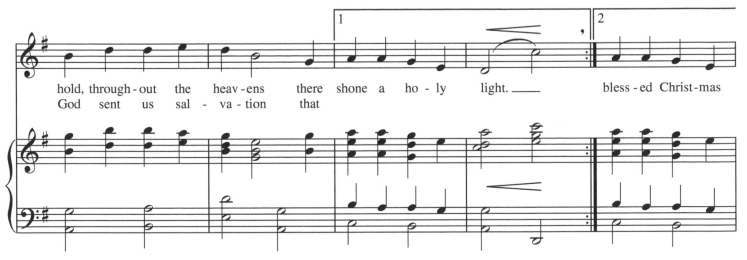

hold, through-out the heav-ens there shone a ho - ly light. _____ bless-ed Christ-mas
God sent us sal - va - tion that

morn. _____ Go, tell it on the moun - tain, o - ver the hills and

ev - 'ry - where. Go, tell it on the moun - tain that Je - sus Christ _ is

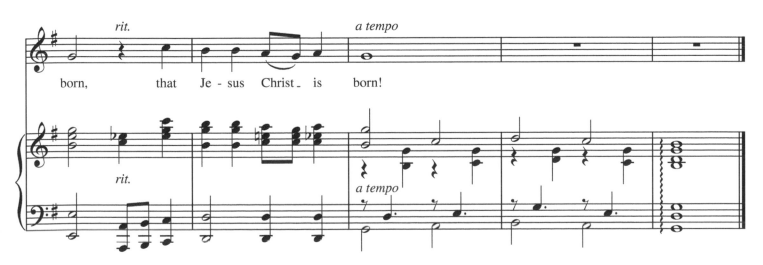

born, that Je - sus Christ _ is born!

The Gospel Train

African-American Spiritual
arranged by Richard Walters

Moderately fast ♩ = c. 160

The gos-pel train is-a-com-in', I hear it just at hand. __ I hear the car __ wheels mov-in' and rum-blin' through the land. __ Oh, get on

board, lit - tle chil - dren, get on board, lit - tle

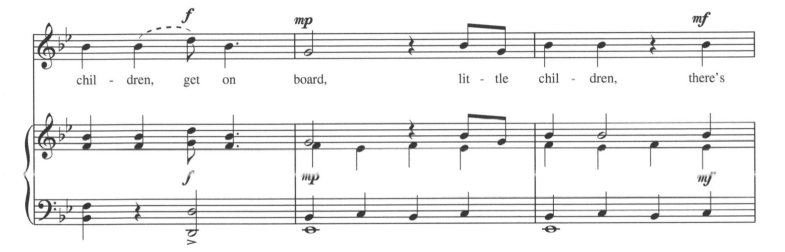

chil - dren, get on board, lit - tle chil - dren, there's

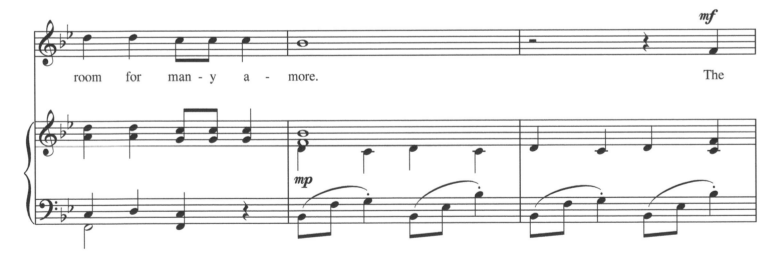

room for man - y a - more. The

fare is cheap and __ all can go, __ the rich and poor are

26

there. __ No sec - ond class __ a - board this train, no

dif - f'rence in the fare. __ Oh, get on board, lit - tle

chil - dren, get on board, lit - tle chil - dren, get on board, lit - tle

chil - dren, there's room for man - y a - more. Oh, get on

board, lit - tle chil - dren, get on board, lit - tle

chil - dren, get on board, lit - tle chil - dren, there's

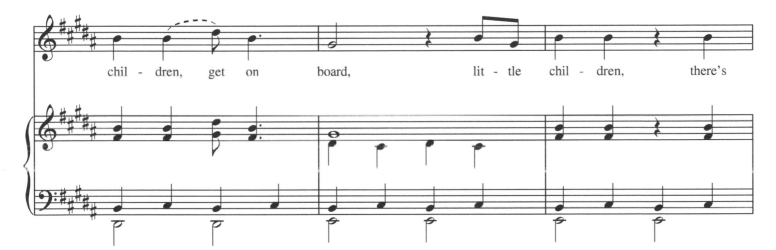

room for man - y a - more, there's room for man - y a -

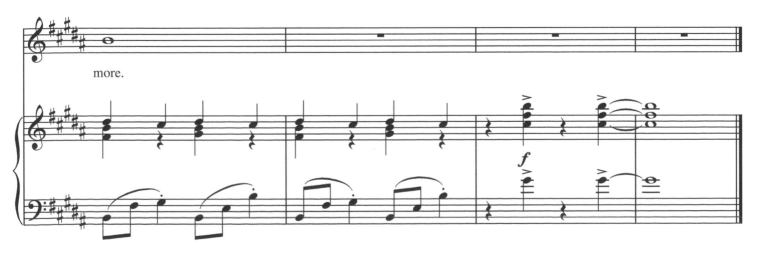

more.

He's Got the Whole World in His Hands

African-American Spiritual
arranged by Joel K. Boyd

in His hands, __ He's got the whole world in His hands. ___
in His hands, __ He's got the whole world in His hands. __
2. He's got the

3. He's got you and me broth - er, ___ in His hands, __ He's got

you and me sis - ter, ___ in His hands, __ He's got you and me broth - er, ___

in His hands, __ He's got the whole world in His hands. __

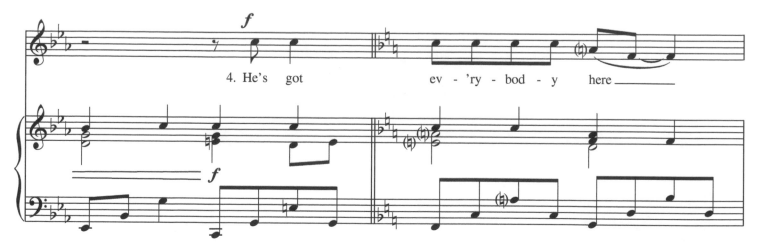

4. He's got ev - 'ry - bod - y here _____

in His hands, ___ He's got ev - 'ry - bod - y here _____

in His hands, ___ He's got ev - 'ry - bod - y here _____

in His hands, ___ He's got the whole world in His hands. __

5. He's got the whole world _____ in His hands, ___ He's got the

whole wide world _____ in His hands, ___ He's got the

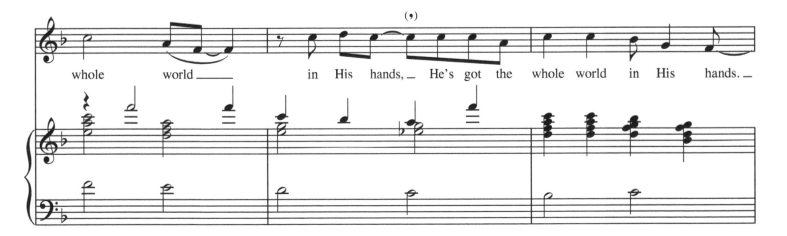

whole world _____ in His hands, ___ He's got the whole world in His hands. ___

He's got the whole world in His hands. ___

Ped.

Let Us Break Bread Together

African-American Spiritual
arranged by Christopher Ruck

Simply, not too slow ♩ = c. 128

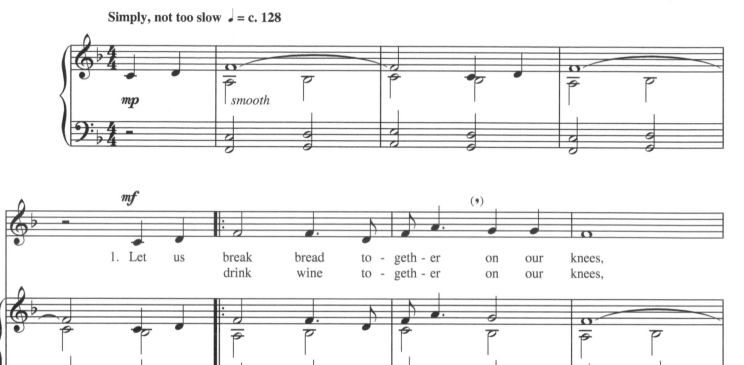

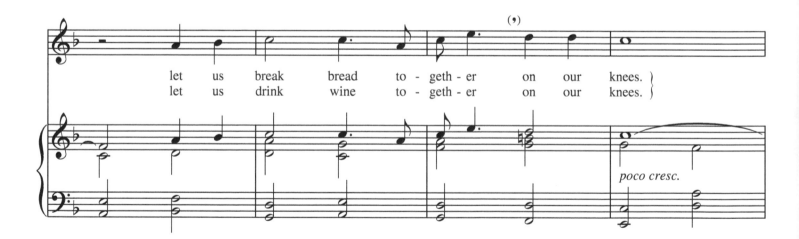

1. Let us break bread to-geth-er on our knees,
drink wine to-geth-er on our knees,

let us break bread to-geth-er on our knees. }
let us drink wine to-geth-er on our knees. }

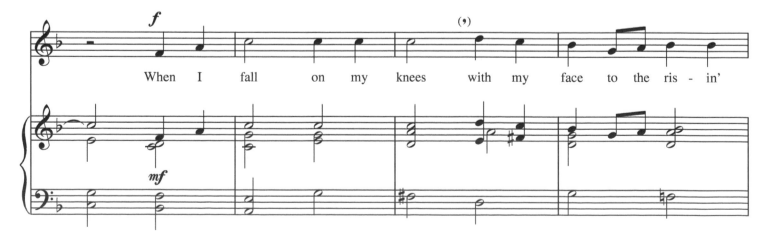

When I fall on my knees with my face to the ris-in'

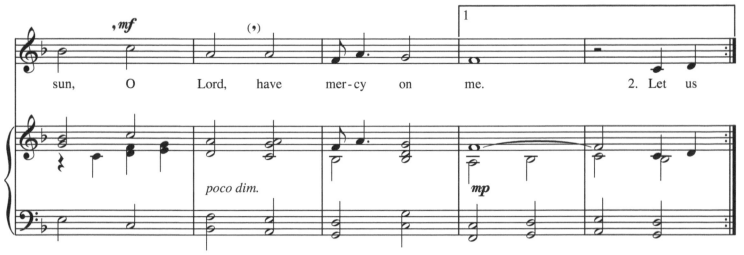

sun, O Lord, have mer-cy on me. 2. Let us

me.

3. Let us praise God to-geth-er on our knees,

let us praise God to-geth-er on our knees.

When I fall on my knees with my face to the ris - in'

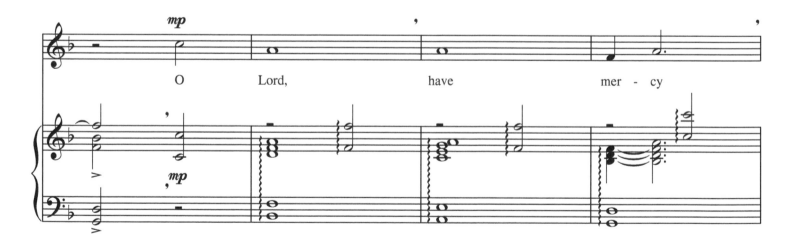

sun, O Lord, have mer - cy on me,

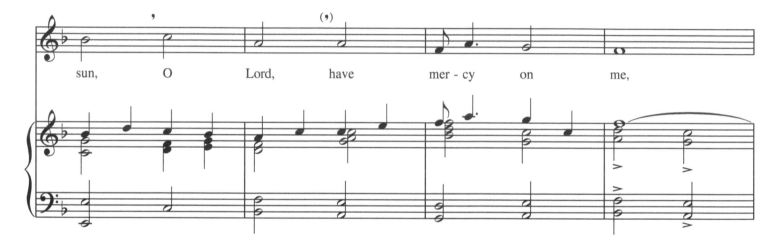

O Lord, have mer - cy

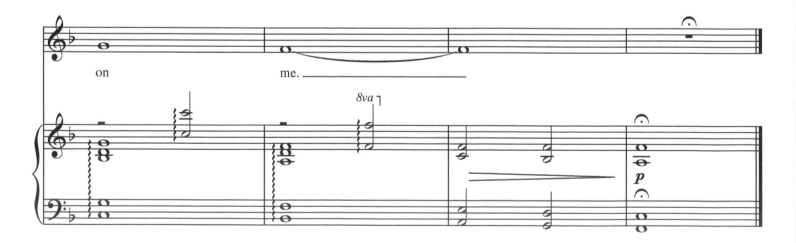

on me.

Lord, I Want to Be a Christian

African-American Spiritual
arranged by Joel K. Boyd

In my heart, in my heart,_____

poco rit. *a tempo*

Lord, I want to be a Chris - tian in my
Lord, I want to be more lov - ing in my

poco rit. *a tempo*

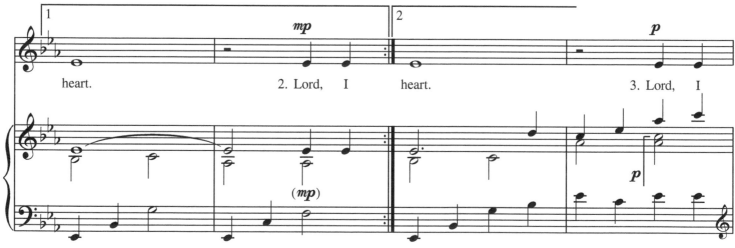

heart. 2. Lord, I heart. 3. Lord, I

want to be like Je - sus in my heart, in my heart.__ Lord, I

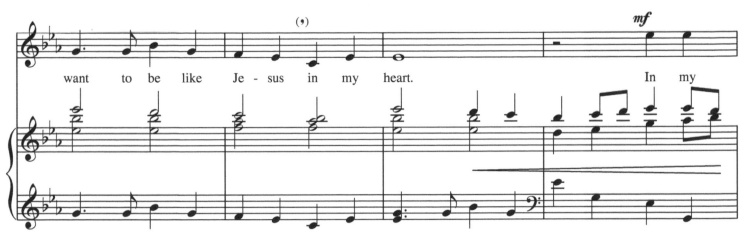

Mary Had a Baby

African-American Spiritual
arranged by Richard Walters

3. Where was he born, — my Lord? Where was he born, — my Lord?

Mar-y had a ba-by, born in a sta-ble. Mar-y had a ba-by, my Lord.

Laid him in a man-ger, my Lord. Laid him in a man-ger,

my Lord. Mar-y had a ba-by, laid him in a man-ger. Mar-y had a ba-by, my Lord.

Sometimes I Feel Like a Motherless Child

African-American Spiritual
arranged by Richard Walters

home, _____ a long way __ from home.

Some - times I feel like I'm al - most gone, __

some - times I feel like I'm al - most gone, __

some - times I feel like I'm al - most gone, __ way

up in the heav-en - ly land, _____ way

up in the heav-en - ly land. Way

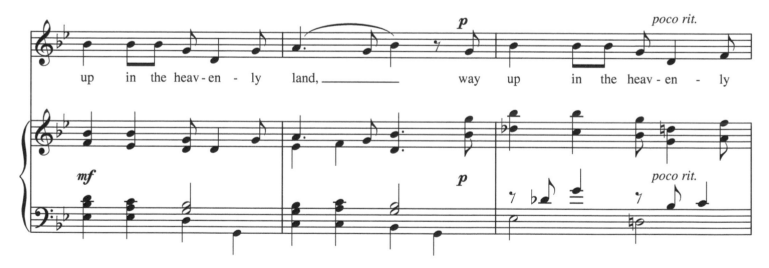

up in the heav-en - ly land, _____ way up in the heav-en - ly

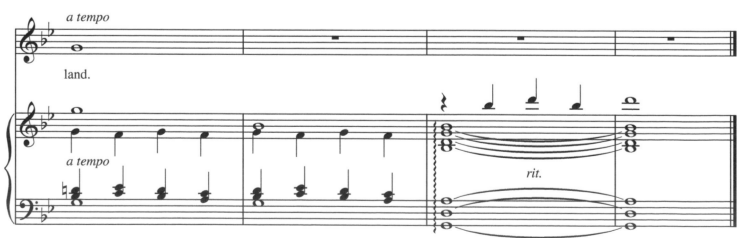

land.

Steal Away

African-American Spiritual
arranged by Christopher Ruck

Moderately ♩ = c. 80

Steal a-way, steal a-way, steal a-way to Je - sus.

Steal a-way, steal a-way home. I ain' got long to stay here.

A little faster ♩ = c. 96

1. My Lord, He calls me, He calls me by the thun - der. }
2. Green trees are bend - in', Poor sin - ners stand a trem - blin'. }

The

Tempo I

trum-pet sounds with-in-a my soul. I ain' got long to stay here.

Steal a - way, steal a - way, steal a - way to Je - sus.

Steal a-way, steal a-way home. I ain' got long to stay here.

A little faster ♩ = c. 96

My Lord, He calls me, He calls me by the light-nin'. The trum-pet sounds with

Tempo I

in - a my soul. I ain' got long to stay here, I

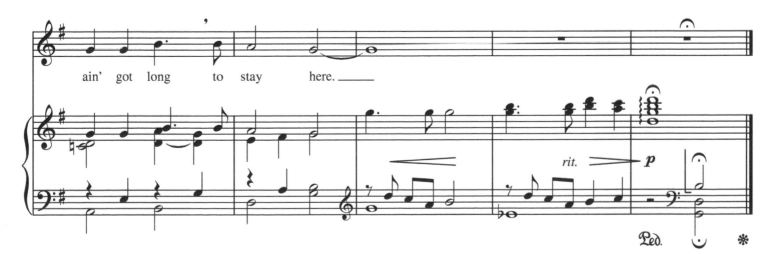

ain' got long to stay here. ____

Swing Low, Sweet Chariot

African-American Spiritual
arranged by Joel K. Boyd

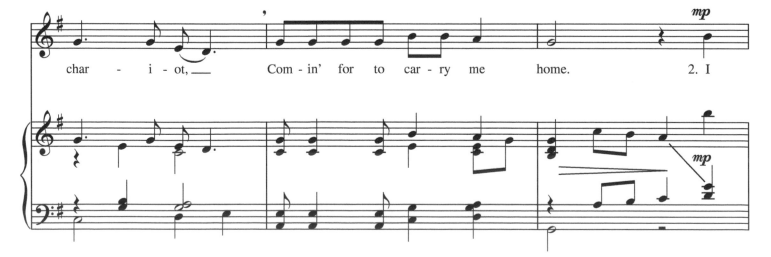

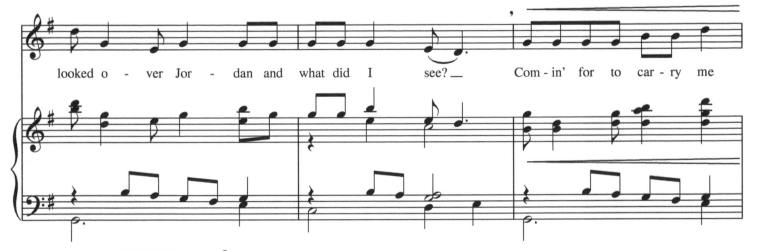

looked o - ver Jor - dan and what did I see? __ Com - in' for to car - ry me

home, A band __ of an - gels com - in' af - ter me, __

Com - in' for to car - ry me home. 3. If you get there be -

fore I do, __ Com - in' for to car - ry me home, Tell

all my friends I'm com - in' too, _ Com - in' for to car - ry me home.

Swing low, sweet char - i - ot, _ Com - in' for to car - ry me home.

Swing _ low, sweet char - i - ot, _ Com - in' for to car - ry me home,

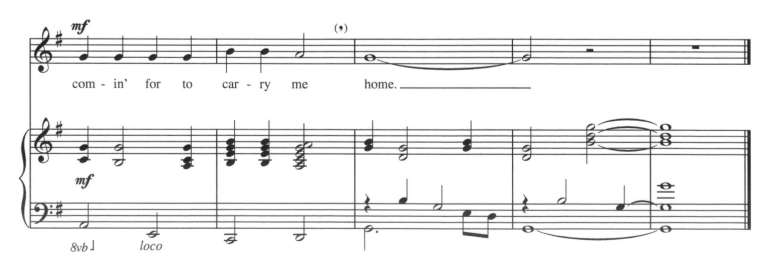

com - in' for to car - ry me home. _____

This Little Light of Mine

African-American Spiritual
arranged by Christopher Ruck

All through the night, I'm gon-na let it shine,

All through the night, I'm gon-na let it shine, let it

shine, let it shine, let it shine!

Ev - 'ry - where I go,

51

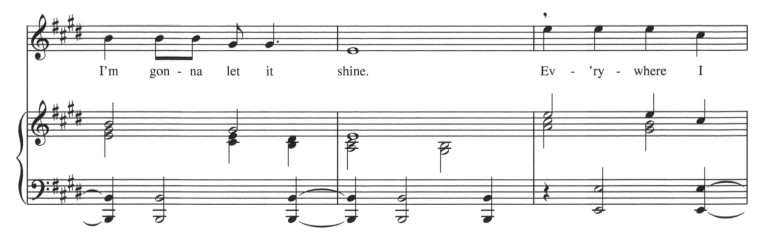

I'm gon-na let it shine. Ev - 'ry - where I

go, I'm gon-na let it shine, let it

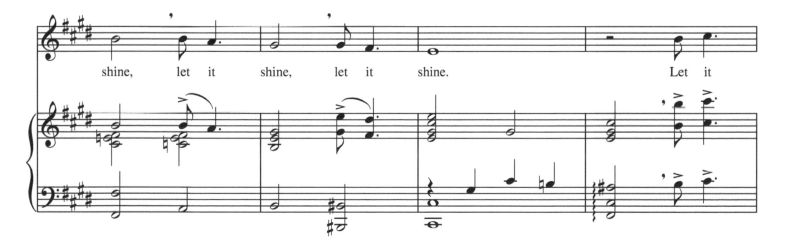

shine, let it shine, let it shine. Let it

shine, let it shine, let it shine!

Were You There?

African-American Spiritual
arranged by Brian Dean

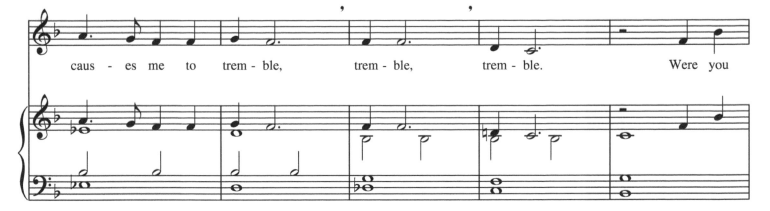

caus - es me to trem - ble, trem - ble, trem - ble. Were you

there when they cru - ci - fied my Lord?

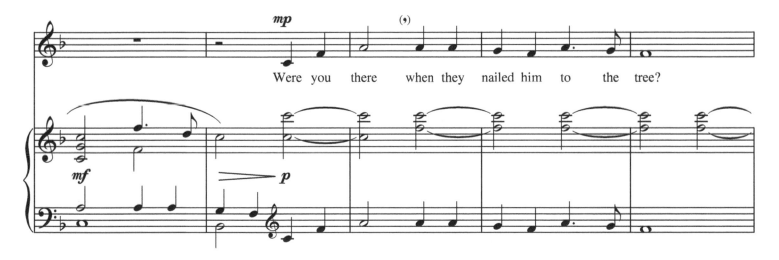

Were you there when they nailed him to the tree?

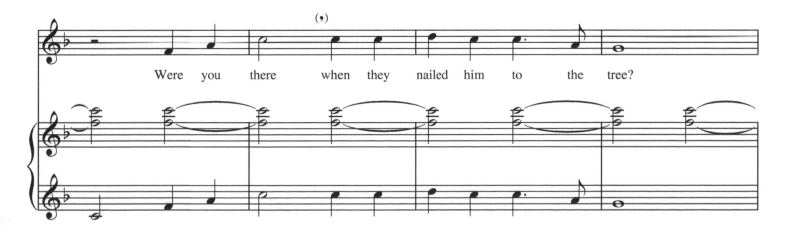

Were you there when they nailed him to the tree?

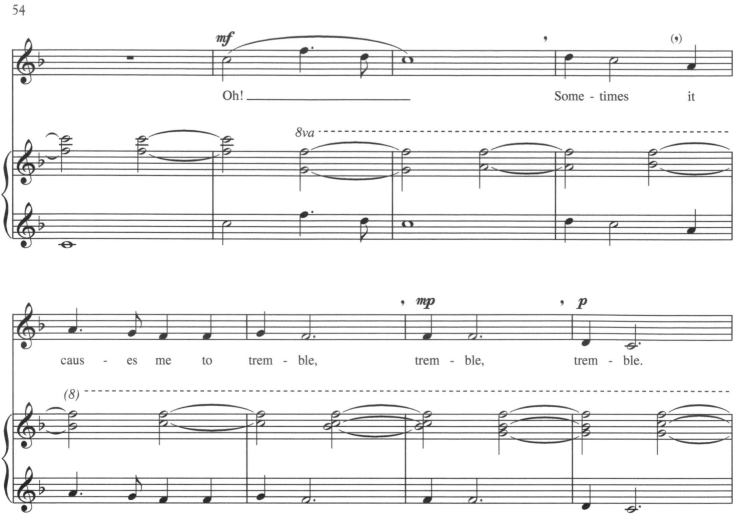

Oh! _____ Some - times it

caus - es me to trem - ble, trem - ble, trem - ble.

Were you there when they nailed him to the tree?

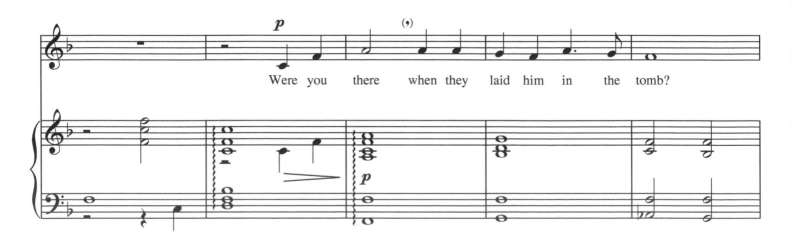

Were you there when they laid him in the tomb?